When Is a Fish Not a Fish?

by Cameron Dokey

MODERN CURRICULUM PRESS
Pearson Learning Group

There is a creature on our planet that lives in every ocean in the world. Some of these creatures have bodies as small as a pea on your dinner plate. Others have bodies as large as basketballs. Some blend in with the ocean around them. Others can glow in the dark like stars.

You may even have seen this creature yourself at the beach—floating in the water or washed up like driftwood on the seashore.

Its name says it is a fish, but that really isn't true.

What is this creature?

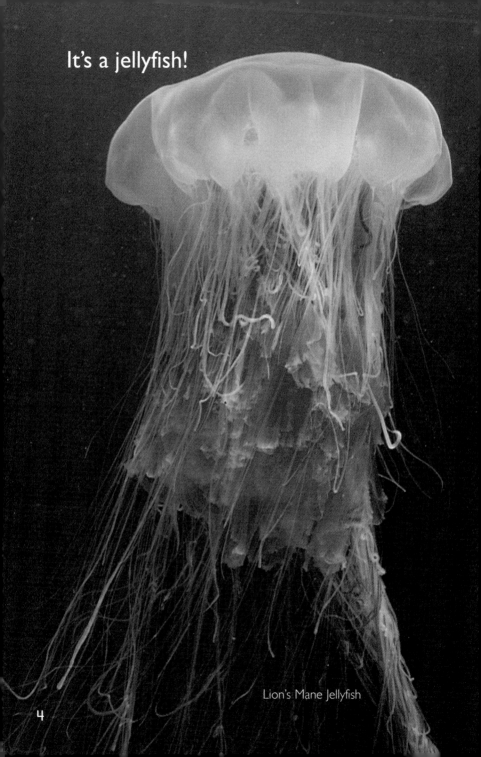

It's a jellyfish!

Lion's Mane Jellyfish

Purple Jellyfish

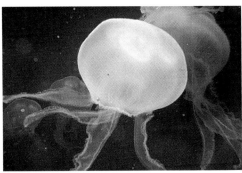

Moon Jellyfish

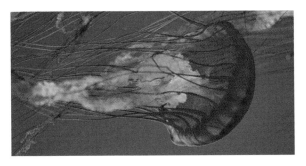

Sea Nettle

Mangrove Jellyfish

A jellyfish isn't a true fish. True fish have fins and gills. We use that name because jellyfish live underwater. The "jelly" in jellyfish is in the animal's upper body. Because of its shape, this part of a jellyfish is called the bell or umbrella.

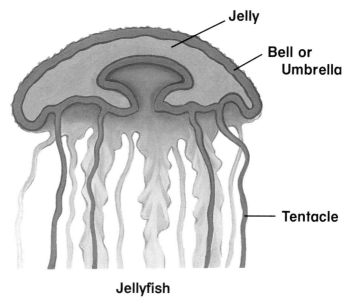

Jelly

Bell or Umbrella

Tentacle

Jellyfish

In fact, you can use an umbrella to get a good idea of how a jellyfish moves through the water. First, open the umbrella, so that you can see how it is shaped like a jellyfish. Now slowly open and close the umbrella.

When a jellyfish opens, it lets water into its bell. When it closes, it pushes the water out and shoots itself through the water.

You have some things a jellyfish doesn't have. One of them is a brain. Another one is a skeleton. Without your hard bones to hold you up, your body would collapse. What holds up a jellyfish's body? The jelly!

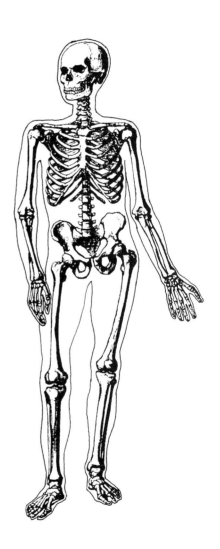

Imagine two balloons floating in the water, one inside the other. Now, imagine that the space between the two balloons is filled with something soft and squishy, just like jelly.

Now you can imagine what a jellyfish's body is like: two layers of cells, like the two layers of balloons, separated by a layer of soft jelly.

But there's more to a jellyfish's body than just jelly. Like you, a jellyfish has to eat. A jellyfish must catch its own food. It is a predator.

To catch its food, or prey, a jellyfish uses its tentacles. The tentacles hang down from the jellyfish's bell.

Some tentacles are thin. Some are short. But no matter what its size, each tentacle is specially designed to catch prey. It is covered with many tiny stinging cells. The stinging cells on a tentacle may be small, but they can deliver a big dose of poison. Stings from a jellyfish can paralyze a fish in just a few seconds.

Portugese Man-of-War with Captured Fish

Colonial Jellyfish

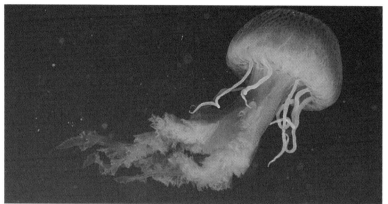

Purple Jellyfish

When a fish brushes against a tentacle, the stinging cells instantly pop open. Each cell shoots a tiny dart into the fish to hook it and hold it in place. Then the jellyfish injects the poison.

The fish struggles. But soon, the struggle is over.

Now the jellyfish moves the captured prey up to its mouth. It's dinnertime.

Fish aren't the only creatures that should be wary of a jellyfish's tentacles. If you brush against some kinds of jellyfish, you might feel a sting too. One of the most dangerous animals in the world is a kind of jellyfish. Its nickname is the sea wasp, and it lives off the coast of Australia. The sting of a sea wasp is so powerful that it can kill a human being in about three minutes!

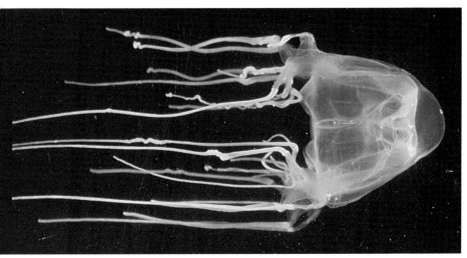

Sea Wasp

Another dangerous sea animal is a close relative of the jellyfish. It's called the Portuguese man-of-war.

Never touch an animal that looks like a jellyfish, not even one washed up on shore. A dead jellyfish can still sting you!

Many fish won't survive a brush with a jellyfish's stinging tentacles. But not all kinds of fish are harmed.

Some fish have skins that are covered by a special coating. These fish can swim right into a jellyfish's mass of tentacles. The special coating on the fish's skin keeps the jellyfish's stinging cells from firing. Fish with this skin often purposely swim into a jellyfish to protect themselves from other kinds of predators.

Portugese Man-of-War.

Some kinds of crabs spend their whole lives living inside the body of a jellyfish. How do they survive? They eat tiny plants growing on the jellyfish. They also eat the jellyfish's leftovers.

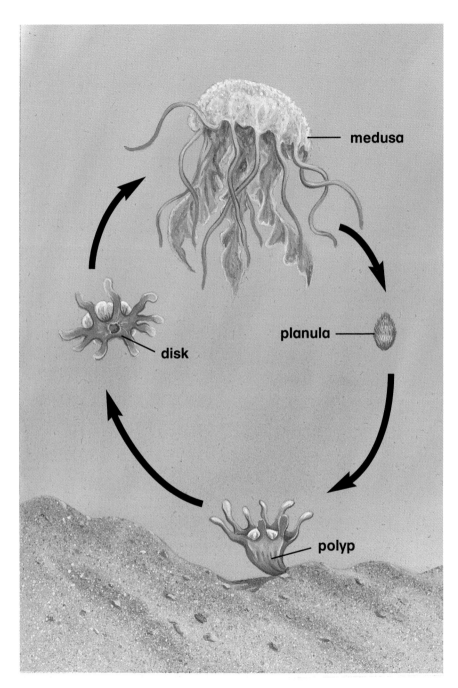

medusa

planula

disk

polyp

A baby jellyfish is a worm-like creature called a planula (PLAN-yoo-luh).

A planula can swim, but mostly it just floats in the water. As time passes, the planula sinks to the bottom. There, it attaches itself to a rock or something else sturdy, like the spar of a sunken ship.

Next, the jellyfish grows into something called a polyp (POL-ip). It is a polyp for about a year. A polyp looks like a tree, but its branches are tentacles that the polyp uses to trap and sting its prey.

A jellyfish can't swim while it's a polyp. But during this time, it is doing something important. It is growing disks.

After about a year, the disks break off and float around. The disks look like snowflakes or stars. A week or so later, each disk becomes a medusa (muh-DOO-suhs). This medusa is now at the jellyfish stage most people recognize.

Many kinds of jellyfish get their names from their appearance.

The thimble jellyfish gets its name from its bell, which is shaped like a sewing thimble. A lion's mane jellyfish gets its name from its yellow- to red-brown color and its thick cluster of long tentacles.

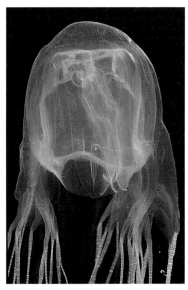
Box Jellyfish

Glass Jellyfish

Lion's Mane Jellyfish